The Words & Wisdom
of
Ben Franklin

R. Scott Frothingham

Quotable Quotes from Ben Franklin

Before we get to the long-form pieces, let's take a look at some of the great "sound bite" quotes attributed to this "larger-than-life" figure from the past.

He that is good for making excuses is seldom good for anything else.

Any fool can criticize, condemn and complain and most fools do.

Either write something worth reading or do something worth writing.

We are all born ignorant, but one must work hard to remain stupid.

The U. S. Constitution doesn't guarantee happiness, only the pursuit of it. You have to catch up with it yourself.

If passion drives you, let reason hold the reins.

If a man empties his purse into his head, no one can take it from him.

He that speaks much, is much mistaken.

You may delay, but time will not.

Beware of little expenses. A small leak will sink a great ship.

A learned blockhead is a greater blockhead than an ignorant one.

Three can keep a secret, if two of them are dead.

Wine is constant proof that God loves us and loves to see us happy.

They who can give up essential liberty to obtain a little temporary safety deserve neither liberty nor safety.

Tell me and I forget. Teach me and I remember. Involve me and I learn.

Guests, like fish, begin to smell after three days.

Money has never made man happy, nor will it, there is nothing in its nature to produce happiness. The more of it one has the more one wants.

Lost time is never found again.

All mankind is divided into three classes: those that are immovable, those that are movable, and those that move.

Honesty is the best policy.

A place for everything, everything in its place.

Life's Tragedy is that we get old too soon and wise too late.

A house is not a home unless it contains food and fire for the mind as well as the body.

Who is wise? He that learns from everyone. Who is powerful? He that governs his passions. Who is rich? He that is content. Who is that? Nobody.

He that would live in peace and at ease must not speak all he knows or all he sees.

Remember not only to say the right thing in the right place, but far more difficult still, to leave unsaid the wrong thing at the tempting moment.

A life of leisure and a life of laziness are two things. There will be sleeping enough in the grave.

Do not fear mistakes. You will know failure. Continue to reach out.

A penny saved is a penny earned.

Having been poor is no shame, but being ashamed of it, is.

He that won't be counseled can't be helped.

Hide not your talents. They for use were made. What's a sundial in the shade?

Genius without education is like silver in the mine.

Keep your eyes wide open before marriage, half shut afterwards.

It is the working man who is the happy man. It is the idle man who is the miserable man.

Content makes poor men rich; discontent makes rich men poor.

It takes many good deeds to build a good reputation, and only one bad one to lose it.

Whatever is begun in anger ends in shame.

Tricks and treachery are the practice of fools, that don't have brains enough to be honest.

How few there are who have courage enough to own their faults, or resolution enough to mend them.

Half a truth is often a great lie.

At twenty years of age the will reigns; at thirty, the wit; and at forty, the judgment.

Most people return small favors, acknowledge medium ones and repay greater ones - with ingratitude.

Energy and persistence conquer all things.

Never leave that till tomorrow which you can do today.

Anger is never without a reason, but seldom with a good one.

When in doubt, don't.

Without continual growth and progress, such words as improvement, achievement, and success have no meaning.

A man wrapped up in himself makes a very small bundle.

An investment in knowledge pays the best interest.

Wise men don't need advice. Fools won't take it.

Work as if you were to live a hundred years. Pray as if you were to die tomorrow.

If you desire many things, many things will seem few.

He who falls in love with himself will have no rivals.

Words may show a man's wit but actions his meaning.

Dost thou love life? Then do not squander time, for that is the stuff life is made of.

There are two ways of being happy: We must either diminish our wants or augment our means - either may do - the result is the same and it is for each man to decide for himself and to do that which happens to be easier.

It is only when the rich are sick that they fully feel the impotence of wealth.

The doorstep to the temple of wisdom is a knowledge of our own ignorance.

If all printers were determined not to print anything till they were sure it would offend nobody, there would be very little printed.

Many people die at twenty five and aren't buried until they are seventy five.

Your net worth to the world is usually determined by what remains after your bad habits are subtracted from your good ones.

Being ignorant is not so much a shame, as being unwilling to learn.

Well done is better than well said.

Who is Silence Dogood?

In 1722 a series of letters poking fun at various aspects of life in colonial America appeared in the *New-England Courant*. Written by a middle-aged widow named Silence Dogood, the letters addressed, among other things, drunkenness, religious hypocrisy, and the persecution of women.

Silence Dogood even gave her opinion that Harvard, having been ruined by corruption and elitism, taught its students only how to be conceited:

> *I reflected in my Mind on the extream Folly of those Parents, who, blind to their Childrens Dulness, and insensible of the Solidity of their Skulls, because they think their Purses can afford it, will needs send them to the Temple of Learning, where, for want of a suitable Genius, they learn little more than how to carry themselves handsomely, and enter a Room genteely, (which might as well be acquir'd at a Dancing-School,) and from whence they return, after Abundance of Trouble and Charge, as great Blockheads as ever, only more proud and self-conceited.*

Silence Dogood was actually the invention of sixteen year-old Benjamin Franklin, who was working as an apprentice in his older brother James' printing shop in Boston, where *The New-England Courant* was printed.

Franklin concealed his authorship of the letters from his brother. He later wrote that he secretly slipped the first Silence Dogood letter beneath the door of his brother's printing shop at night and later enjoyed listening in to his brother and his friends discussing the letter and making the decision to include it on the front page of the paper.

Franklin wrote a total of fourteen Silence Dogood letters between April 2 to October 8, 1722 and when he stopped writing the letters, his brother placed an ad in the paper in an attempt to find out who the mysterious letter writer really was:

> *If any person or persons will give a true account of Mrs. Silence Dogood, whether dead or alive, married or unmarried, in town or countrey, that so, (if living) she may be spoke with, or letters convey'd to her, they shall have thanks for their pains.*

When Franklin confessed to his brother that he was Silence Dogood, James was extremely displeased. Soon thereafter, Franklin left his apprenticeship -- without permission -- running away to seek his fortune in Philadelphia.

> NOTE: In the 2004 movie, National Treasure, the Silence Dogood letters are represented as the basis for a secret code that, when solved, would lead to the site of a hidden treasure trove.

Here is the 13th letter from Silence Dogood:

To the author of the New England Courant.

SIR,

In Persons of a contemplative Disposition, the most indifferent Things provoke the Exercise of the Imagination; and the Satisfactions which often arise to them thereby, are a certain Relief to the Labour of the Mind (when it has been intensely fix'd on more substantial Subjects) as well as to that of the Body.

In one of the late pleasant Moon-light Evenings, I so far indulg'd in my self the Humour of the Town in walking abroad, as to continue from my Lodgings two or three Hours later than usual, & was pleas'd beyond Expectation before my Return. Here I found various Company to observe, and various Discourse to attend to. I met indeed with the common Fate of *Listeners*, (who *hear no good of themselves*,) but from a Consciousness of my Innocence, receiv'd it with a Satisfaction beyond what the Love of Flattery and the Daubings of a Parasite could produce. The Company who rally'd me were about Twenty in Number, of both Sexes; and tho' the *Confusion of Tongues* (like that of *Babel*) which always happens among so many impetuous Talkers, render'd their Discourse not so intelligible as I could wish, I learnt thus much, That one of the Females pretended to know me, from some Discourse she had heard at a certain House before the Publication of one of my Letters; adding, *That I was a Person of an ill Character, and kept a criminal Correspondence with a Gentleman who assisted me in Writing.* One of the Gallants clear'd me of this random Charge, by saying, *That tho' I wrote in the Character of a Woman, he knew me to be a Man; But,* continu'd he, *he has more need of endeavouring a Reformation in himself, than spending his Wit in satyrizing others.*

I had no sooner left this Set of Ramblers, but I met a Crowd of *Tarpolins* and their Doxies, link'd to each other by the Arms, who ran (by their own Account) after the Rate of *Six Knots an Hour*, and bent their Course towards the *Common*. Their eager and amorous Emotions of Body, occasion'd by taking their Mistresses *in Tow*, they call'd *wild Steerage*: And as a Pair of them happen'd to trip and come to the Ground, the Company were call'd upon to *bring to*, for that *Jack* and *Betty* were *founder'd*. But this Fleet were not less comical or irregular in their Progress than a Company of Females I soon after came up with, who, by throwing their Heads to the Right and Left, at every one who pass'd by them, I concluded came out with no other Design than to revive the Spirit of Love in Disappointed Batchelors, and expose themselves to Sale to the first Bidder.

But it would take up too much Room in your Paper to mention all the Occasions of Diversion I met with in this Night's Ramble. As it grew later, I observed, that many pensive Youths with down Looks and a slow Pace, would be ever now and then crying out on the Cruelty of their Mistresses; others with a more rapid Pace and chearful Air, would be swinging their Canes, and clapping their Cheeks, and whispering at certain Intervals, *I'm certain I shall have her! This is more than I expected! How charmingly she talks!* &c.;

Upon the whole I conclude, That our *Night-Walkers* are a Set of People, who contribute very much to the Health and Satisfaction of those who have been fatigu'd with Business or Study, and occasionally observe their pretty Gestures and impertinencies. But among Men of Business, the *Shoemakers,* and other Dealers in Leather, are doubly oblig'd to them, inasmuch as they exceedingly promote the Consumption of their Ware: And I have heard of a *Shoemaker,* who being ask'd by a noted Rambler, *Whether he could tell how long her Shoeswould last*; very prettily answer'd, *That he knew how many Days she might wear them, but not how many Nights; because they were then put to a more violent and irregular Service than when she employ'd her self in the common Affairs of the House.*

I am, SIR,
Your Humble Servant,
SILENCE DOGOOD.

The New-England Courant, September 24, 1722

Thirteen Virtues

In his autobiography, Franklin lists a plan of 13 virtues that he developed at age 20 and practiced in some form for the remainder of his life. He would pick one to work on each week "leaving all others to their ordinary chance." Although he admitted that he fell short of living by his virtues, Franklin believed the attempt made him a better man. In his autobiography he wrote, "I hope, therefore, that some of my descendants may follow the example and reap the benefit."

1. "Temperance. Eat not to dullness; drink not to elevation."

2. "Silence. Speak not but what may benefit others or yourself; avoid trifling conversation."

3. "Order. Let all your things have their places; let each part of your business have its time."

4. "Resolution. Resolve to perform what you ought; perform without fail what you resolve."

5. "Frugality. Make no expense but to do good to others or yourself; i.e., waste nothing."

6. "Industry. Lose no time; be always employ'd in something useful; cut off all unnecessary actions."

7. "Sincerity. Use no hurtful deceit; think innocently and justly, and, if you speak, speak accordingly."

8. "Justice. Wrong none by doing injuries, or omitting the benefits that are your duty."

9. "Moderation. Avoid extremes; forbear resenting injuries so much as you think they deserve."

10. "Cleanliness. Tolerate no uncleanliness in body, cloaths, or habitation."

11. "Tranquility. Be not disturbed at trifles, or at accidents common or unavoidable."

12. "Chastity. Rarely use venery but for health or offspring, never to dullness, weakness, or the injury of your own or another's peace or reputation."

13. "Humility. Imitate Jesus and Socrates."

Speech at the Conclusion of the Constitutional Convention

Prior to the signing of the final draft of the Constitution on the last day of the Constitutional Convention (9/17/1787), Pennsylvania delegate Franklin wanted to give a speech. He was too weak to give the speech himself, so he had fellow Pennsylvanian James Wilson deliver it. Many consider it a masterpiece.

Mr. President

I confess that there are several parts of this constitution which I do not at present approve, but I am not sure I shall never approve them: For having lived long, I have experienced many instances of being obliged by better information, or fuller consideration, to change opinions even on important subjects, which I once thought right, but found to be otherwise. It is therefore that the older I grow, the more apt I am to doubt my own judgment, and to pay more respect to the judgment of others. Most men indeed as well as most sects in Religion, think themselves in possession of all truth, and that wherever others differ from them it is so far error. Steele a Protestant in a Dedication tells the Pope, that the only difference between our Churches in their opinions of the certainty of their doctrines is, the Church of Rome is infallible and the Church of England is never in the wrong. But though many private persons think almost as highly of their own infallibility as of that of their sect, few express it so naturally as a certain french lady, who in a dispute with her sister, said "I don't know how it happens, Sister but I meet with no body but myself, that's always in the right — *Il n'y a que moi qui a toujours raison.*"

In these sentiments, Sir, I agree to this Constitution with all its faults, if they are such; because I think a general Government necessary for us, and there is no form of Government but what may be a blessing to the people if well administered, and believe farther that this is likely to be well administered for a course of years, and can only end in Despotism, as other forms have done before it, when the people shall become so corrupted as to need despotic Government, being incapable of any other. I doubt too whether any other Convention we can obtain, may be able to make a better Constitution. For when you assemble a number of men to have the advantage of their joint wisdom, you inevitably assemble with those men, all their prejudices, their passions, their errors of opinion, their local interests, and their selfish views. From such an assembly can a perfect production be expected? It therefore astonishes me, Sir, to find this system approaching so near to perfection as it does; and I think it will astonish our enemies, who are waiting with confidence to hear that our councils are confounded like those of the Builders of Babel; and that our States are on the point of separation, only to meet hereafter for the purpose of cutting one another's throats. Thus I consent, Sir, to this Constitution because I expect no better, and because I am not sure, that it is not the best. The opinions I have had of its errors, I sacrifice to the public good. I have never whispered a syllable of them abroad. Within these walls they were born, and here they shall die. If every one of us in returning to our Constituents were to report the objections he has had to it, and endeavor to gain partizans in support of them, we might prevent its being generally received, and thereby lose all the salutary effects & great advantages resulting naturally in our favor among foreign Nations as well as among ourselves, from our real or apparent unanimity. Much of the strength & efficiency of any Government in procuring and securing happiness to the people, depends, on opinion, on the general opinion of the goodness of the Government, as well as of the wisdom and integrity of its Governors. I hope therefore that for our own sakes as a part of the people, and for the sake of posterity, we shall act heartily and unanimously in recommending this Constitution (if approved by Congress & confirmed by the Conventions) wherever our influence may extend, and turn our future thoughts & endeavors to the means of having it well administred.

On the whole, Sir, I can not help expressing a wish that every member of the Convention who may still have objections to it, would with me, on this occasion doubt a little of his own infallibility, and to make manifest our unanimity, put his name to this instrument.

Benjamin Franklin's Imaginary Speech

On February 7, 1775, Franklin published "An Imaginary Speech" defending American courage in *The Public Advertiser*, as a response to a British officer's comments to Parliament that the British should not fear the colonial rebels, because "Americans are unequal to the People of this Country [Britain] in Devotion to Women, and in Courage, and worse than all, they are religious."

An Imaginary Speech

To the Printer of the Public Advertiser.

SIR, In a late Debate, a certain North British Colonel thought proper to recommend himself to the Court, by grossly abusing the Americans. I send you the Answer I should have made to him had I been present when he uttered his Invective, and I rely upon it, that you will shew that Candour and Justice to America which is refused in certain great Assemblies, and not condemn them without a Hearing.

Mr. Sp ------ r, Sir, I am an American: In that Character I trust this House will shew some little Indulgence to the Feelings which are excited by what fell this Moment from an honourable and military Gentleman under the Gallery. According to him, Sir, the Americans are unequal to the People of this Country in Devotion to Women, and in Courage, and in what, in his Sight seems worse than all, they are religious.

No one, Sir, feels the Odiousness of Comparisons more than myself. But I am necessitated to pursue, in some measure, the

Path which the honourable Gentleman has marked out. Sir, let the rapid Increase and Population of America, compared with the Decrease of England and of Scotland, shew which of the two People are most effectually devoted to the Fair Sex. The Americans are content to leave with that honourable Gentleman and his Companions the Boast, while the Fact is evidently with them. They are sensible, that upon this Subject to talk much, and to do little, are inseparable.

Sir, I am at a Loss to conceive upon what Facts the Gentleman grounds his Impeachment of American Courage. Is it upon the Capture of Louisbourg, and the Conquest of Nova Scotia in the War before the last? Is it upon their having alone taken Crown Point from the French Regulars, and made their General Prisoner, or from their having covered the Retreat of the British Regulars, and saved them from utter Destruction in the Expeditions under Braddock, and to Fort Pitt?

Sir, it happens very unfortunately that the Regulars have impressed the Provincials with a very indifferent Opinion of their Courage. I will tell you why. They saw General Braddock at the Head of a regular Army march with a Thousand Boastings of their Courage and Superiority, and expressing the most sovereign Contempt of the Virginian Provincials who accompanied him. But in a little Time these vain Boasters were totally routed by a very unequal Number of French and Indians, and the Provincials rendered them the unthanked Service of saving them from being cut off to a Man. In the same Manner a Detachment of Highlanders, under a Major Grant, accompanied by the Virginians under Major Lewis, being attacked by the Indians, the Highlanders fled immediately, and left the Provincials to retreat and cover them. They saw several Campaigns of shameful Defeats, or as shameful Inactivity: Till at length the all-pervading Spirit of one great Officer, and the cautious Abilities of another, redeemed the British Name, and led her Sons to Conquest. The Expedition under Colonel Bouquet, assisted by a large Body of Provincials, owed its Success chiefly to those Provincials. I speak it from that brave Officer's own Letters. It was Wolfe, Amherst and Bouquet who roused the Spirit of the Regulars, and led them to Glory and Success; and I am proud to say, Sir, these are not the Men who traduce the Americans, or speak slightly of their Services; nay more, Sir, the Men who disgraced the Regulars are those only who defame the Provincials. But why should any Gentleman talk in general Terms of their wanting Spirit? Indiscriminate Accusations against the Absent are cowardly Calumnies. Will the Gentleman come to Particulars? Will he name the American he has insulted with Impunity? Who is the provincial Officer who turned his Back in the Day of Battle? There is hardly a Day or an Hour, in which the Honourable Gentleman does not meet with an American. Does he insult any one of them with Impunity? Has he, or will he put their Spirit to the Proof? Till he has done that, Silence, I am sure, will do more Honour to his own.

The Honourable Gentleman says, the Regulars treated the Provincials *as Beasts of Burthen.* There are many of the Provincial Officers in this Town: I have the Honour of knowing them; and I can assure this House, that no Man living would say as much to their Face with Impunity. The Americans, Sir, are well satisfied, that the Ministry intend to make Beasts of Burthen of them. They tell you, however, they will not be Hewers of Wood and Drawers of Water for any Men upon Earth: The Object of this Motion is to compel them. It is my Duty to say, they will and ought to resist such an Attempt; and that if I were there, I should do it without a Moment's Hesitation.

I had almost forgot the Honourable Gentleman's Charge of their being too religious. Sir, they were such Religionists, that vindicated this Country from the Tyranny of the Stuarts. Perhaps the Honourable Gentleman may have some compassionate Feelings for that unhappy Family: Does that sharpen his Resentment against the Americans; who inherit from those Ancestors, not only the same Religion, but the same Love of Liberty and Spirit to defend it?

The Public Advertiser, February 7, 1775

they hear of his rising so early; and especially when I assure them, *that he gives light as soon as he rises.* I am convinced of this. I am certain of my fact. One cannot be more certain of any fact. I saw it with my own eyes. And, having repeated this observation the three following mornings, I found always precisely the same result.

Yet it so happens, that when I speak of this discovery to others, I can easily perceive by their countenances, though they forbear expressing it in words, that they do not quite believe me. One, indeed, who is a learned natural philosopher, has assured me that I must certainly be mistaken as to the circumstance of the light coming into my room; for it being well known, as he says, that there could be no light abroad at that hour, it follows that none could enter from without; and that of consequence, my windows being accidentally left open, instead of letting in the light, had only served to let out the darkness; and he used many ingenious arguments to show me how I might, by that means, have been deceived. I owned that he puzzled me a little, but he did not satisfy me; and the subsequent observations I made, as above mentioned, confirmed me in my first opinion.

This event has given rise in my mind to several serious and important reflections. I considered that, if I had not been awakened so early in the morning, I should have slept six hours longer by the light of the sun, and in exchange have lived six hours the following night by candle-light; and, the latter being a much more expensive light than the former, my love of economy induced me to muster up what little arithmetic I was master of, and to make some calculations, which I shall give you, after observing that utility is, in my opinion the test of value in matters of invention, and that a discovery which can be applied to no use, or is not good for something, is good for nothing.

I took for the basis of my calculation the supposition that there are one hundred thousand families in Paris, and that these families consume in the night half a pound of bougies, or candles, per hour. I think this is a moderate allowance, taking one family with another; for though I believe some consume less, I know that many consume a great deal more. Then estimating seven hours per day as the medium quantity between the time of the sun's rising and ours, he rising during the six following months from six to eight hours before noon, and there being seven hours of course per night in which we burn candles, the account will stand thus;--

In the six months between the 20th of March and the 20th of
September, there are

Nights 183

Hours of each night in which
we burn candles 7

Multiplication gives for the
total number of hours 1,281

These 1,281 hours multiplied
by 100,000, the number of
inhabitants, give 128,100,000

One hundred twenty-eight
millions and one hundred
thousand hours, spent at
Paris by candle-light, which,
at half a pound of wax and
tallow per hour, gives the
weight of 64,050,000

Sixty-four millions and fifty
thousand of pounds, which,
estimating the whole at-the
medium price of thirty sols
the pound, makes the sum of
ninety-six millions and
seventy-five thousand livres
tournois 96,075,000

An immense sum! that the city of Paris might save every year, by the economy of using sunshine instead of candles. If it should be said, that people are apt to be obstinately attached to old customs, and that it will be difficult to induce them to rise before noon, consequently my discovery can be of little use; I answer, *Nil desperandum. I* believe all who have common sense, as soon as they have learnt from this paper that it is daylight when the sun rises, will contrive to rise with him; and, to compel the rest, I would propose the following regulations; First. Let a tax be laid of a louis per window, on every window that is provided with shutters to keep out the light of the sun.

Second. Let the same salutary operation of police be made use of, to prevent our burning candles, that inclined us last winter to be more economical in burning wood; that is, let guards be placed in the shops of the wax and tallow chandlers, and no family be permitted to be supplied with more than one pound of candles per week.

Third. Let guards also be posted to stop all the coaches, &c. that would pass the streets after sunset, except those of physicians, surgeons, and midwives.

Fourth. Every morning, as soon as the sun rises, let all the bells in every church be set ringing; and if that is not sufficient?, let cannon be fired in every street, to wake the sluggards effectually, and make them open their eyes to see their true interest.

All the difficulty will be in the first two or three days; after which the reformation will be as natural and easy as the present irregularity; for, *ce n'est que le premier pas qui coûte.* Oblige a man to rise at four in the morning, and it is more than probable he will go willingly to bed at eight in the evening; and, having had eight hours sleep, he will rise more willingly at four in the morning following. But this sum of ninety-six millions and seventy-five thousand livres is not the whole of what may be saved by my economical project. You may observe, that I have calculated upon only one half of the year, and much may be saved in the other, though the days are shorter. Besides, the immense stock of wax and tallow left unconsumed during the summer, will probably make candles much cheaper for the ensuing winter, and continue them cheaper as long as the proposed reformation shall be supported.

For the great benefit of this discovery, thus freely communicated and bestowed by me on the public, I demand neither place, pension, exclusive privilege, nor any other reward whatever. I expect only to have the honour of it. And yet I know there are little, envious minds, who will, as usual, deny me this and say, that my invention was known to the ancients, and perhaps they may bring passages out of the old books in proof of it. I will not dispute with these people, that the ancients knew not the sun would rise at certain hours; they possibly had, as we have, almanacs that predicted it; but it does not follow thence, that they knew *he gave light as soon as he rose*. This is what I claim as my discovery. If the ancients knew it, it might have been long since forgotten; for it certainly was unknown to the moderns, at least to the Parisians, which to prove, I need use but one plain simple argument. They are as well instructed judicious, and prudent a people as exist anywhere in the world all professing, like myself, to be lovers of economy; and,from the many heavy taxes required from them by the necessitities of the state, have surely an abundant reason to be economical. I say it is impossible that so sensible a people, under such circumstances, should have lived so long by the smoky, unwholesome, and enormously expensive light of candles, if they had really known, that they might have had as much pure light of the sun for nothing. I am, &c.

A SUBSCRIBER

Furious Franklin

Even though the following letter to William Strahan -- a British Member of Parliament and Franklin's friend of 30 years -- was never sent, it demonstrates Franklin's passion and offers an extraordinarily clever Franklin-esque closing.

Philada. July 5. 1775

Mr. Strahan

You are a Member of Parliament, and one of that Majority which has doomed my Country to Destruction. You have begun to burn our Towns and murder our People. — Look upon your hands! They are stained with the Blood of your Relations! — You and I were long Friends:— You are now my Enemy, — and

I am,

Yours.

B. Franklin

Fart Proudly

While he was living abroad as United States Ambassador to France (circa 1781) Franklin wrote "A Letter To A Royal Academy", an essay on flatulence which is also known as "Fart Proudly".

Franklin reportedly felt that the various academic societies in Europe were pretentious and focused on the impractical and wrote this piece in response to a call for scientific papers from the Royal Academy of Brussels.

> NOTE: This was never actually submitted; it was sent to Welsh philosopher Richard Price with whom Franklin often corresponded.

"A Letter To A Royal Academy"

GENTLEMEN,

I have perused your late mathematical Prize Question, proposed in lieu of one in Natural Philosophy, for the ensuing year, viz. *"Une figure quelconque donnee, on demande d'y inscrire le plus grand nombre de fois possible une autre figure plus-petite quelconque, qui est aussi donnee"*. I was glad to find by these following Words, *"l'Acadeemie a jugee que cette deecouverte, en eetendant les bornes de nos connoissances, ne seroit pas sans UTILITE"*, that you esteem *Utility* an essential Point in your Enquiries, which has not always been the case with all Academies; and I conclude therefore that you have given this Question instead of a philosophical, or as the Learned express it, a physical one, because you could not at the time think of a physical one that promis'd greater *Utility*.

Permit me then humbly to propose one of that sort for your consideration, and through you, if you approve it, for the serious Enquiry of learned Physicians, Chemists, &c. of this enlightened Age.

It is universally well known, That in digesting our common Food, there is created or produced in the Bowels of human Creatures, a great Quantity of Wind.

That the permitting this Air to escape and mix with the Atmosphere, is usually offensive to the Company, from the fetid Smell that accompanies it.

That all well-bred People therefore, to avoid giving such Offence, forcibly restrain the Efforts of Nature to discharge that Wind.

That so retain'd contrary to Nature, it not only gives frequently great present Pain, but occasions future Diseases, such as habitual Cholics, Ruptures, Tympanies, &c. often destructive of the Constitution, & sometimes of Life itself.

Were it not for the odiously offensive Smell accompanying such Escapes, polite People would probably be under no more Restraint in discharging such Wind in Company, than they are in spitting, or in blowing their Noses.

My Prize Question therefore should be, *To discover some Drug wholesome & not disagreable, to be mix'd with our common Food, or Sauces, that shall render the natural Discharges of Wind from our Bodies, not only inoffensive, but agreable as Perfumes.*

That this is not a chimerical Project, and altogether impossible, may appear from these Considerations. That we already have some Knowledge of Means capable of *Varying* that Smell. He that dines on stale Flesh, especially with much Addition of Onions, shall be able to afford a Stink that no Company can tolerate; while he that has lived for some Time on Vegetables only, shall have that Breath so pure as to be insensible to the most delicate Noses; and if he can manage so as to avoid the Report, he may any where give Vent to his Griefs, unnoticed. But as there are many to whom an entire Vegetable Diet would be inconvenient, and as a little Quick-Lime thrown into a Jakes will correct the amazing Quantity of fetid Air arising from the vast Mass of putrid Matter contain'd in such Places, and render it rather pleasing to the Smell, who knows but that a little Powder of Lime (or some other thing equivalent) taken in our Food, or perhaps a Glass of Limewater drank at Dinner, may have the same Effect on the Air produc'd in and issuing from our Bowels? This is worth the Experiment. Certain it is also that we have the Power of changing by slight Means the Smell of another Discharge, that of our Water. A few Stems of Asparagus eaten, shall give our Urine a disagreable Odour; and a Pill of Turpentine no bigger than a Pea, shall bestow on it the pleasing Smell of Violets. And why should it be thought more impossible in Nature, to find Means of making a Perfume of our *Wind* than of our *Water*?

For the Encouragement of this Enquiry, (from the immortal Honour to be reasonably expected by the Inventor) let it be considered of how small Importance to Mankind, or to how small a Part of Mankind have been useful those Discoveries in Science that have heretofore made Philosophers famous. Are there twenty Men in Europe at this Day, the happier, or even the easier, for any Knowledge they have pick'd out of Aristotle? What Comfort can the Vortices of Descartes give to a Man who has Whirlwinds in his Bowels! The Knowledge of Newton's mutual *Attraction* of the Particles of Matter, can it afford Ease to him who is rack'd by their mutual *Repulsion*, and the cruel Distensions it occasions? The Pleasure arising to a few Philosophers, from seeing, a few Times in their Life, the Threads of Light untwisted, and separated by the Newtonian

Prism into seven Colours, can it be compared with the Ease and Comfort every Man living might feel seven times a Day, by discharging freely the Wind from his Bowels? Especially if it be converted into a Perfume: For the Pleasures of one Sense being little inferior to those of another, instead of pleasing the *Sight* he might delight the *Smell* of those about him, & make Numbers happy, which to a benevolent Mind must afford infinite Satisfaction. The generous Soul, who now endeavours to find out whether the Friends he entertains like best Claret or Burgundy, Champagne or Madeira, would then enquire also whether they chose Musk or Lilly, Rose or Bergamot, and provide accordingly. And surely such a Liberty of *Expressing* one's *Scent-iments*, and *pleasing one another*, is of infinitely more Importance to human Happiness than that Liberty of the *Press*, or of *abusing one another*, which the English are so ready to fight & die for. -- In short, this Invention, if compleated, would be, as *Bacon* expresses it, *bringing Philosophy home to Mens Business and Bosoms*. And I cannot but conclude, that in Comparison therewith, for *universal*and *continual UTILITY*, the Science of the Philosophers above-mentioned, even with the Addition, Gentlemen, of your *"Figure quelconque"* and the Figures inscrib'd in it, are, all together, scarcely worth a

FART-HING.

Advice to a Friend on Choosing a Mistress

Considered too licentious, this letter from Franklin to Cadwallader Colden – dated June 25, 1745 – was not published in U.S. collections of Franklin's papers for many years. Then, in the mid- to late-20th century it was cited as an example of why obscenity laws should be overturned. Nobody knows whether Franklin was being serious in the letter or if the letter was ever delivered.

My dear Friend:

I know of no medicine fit to diminish the violent natural inclinations you mention; and if I did, I think I should not communicate it to you. Marriage is the proper remedy. It is the most natural state of man, and therefore the state in which you are most likely to find solid happiness. Your reasons against entering into it at present appear to me not well founded. The circumstantial advantages you have in view by postponing it are not only uncertain, but they are small in comparison with that of the thing itself, that being married and settled. It is the man and woman united that make the complete human being. Separate, she wants his force of body and strength of reason; he, her softness, sensibility, and acute discernment. Together they are more likely to succeed in the world. A single man has not nearly the value he would have in the state of union. He is an incomplete animal. He resembles the odd half of a pair of scissors. If you get a prudent, healthy wife, your industry in your profession, with her good economy, will be a fortune sufficient.

But if you will not take the counsel and persist in thinking of a commerce with the sex inevitable, then I repeat my former advice, that in all your amours you should prefer old women to young ones. You call this a paradox and demand my reasons. They are these:

1. Because They have more knowledge of the world, and their minds are better stored with observations, their conversation is more improving and more lastingly agreeable.

2. Because when women cease to be handsome they study to be good. To maintain their influence over men, they supply the diminution of beauty by an augmentation of utility. They learn to do a thousand services small and great, and are the most tender and useful of friends when you are sick. Thus they continue amiable And hence there is hardly such a thing to be found as an old woman who is not a good woman.

3. Because there is no hazard of children, which irregularly produced may be attended with much inconvenience.

4. Because through more experience they are more prudent and discreet in conducting an intrigue to prevent suspicion. The commerce with them is therefore safer with regard to your reputation. And with regard to theirs, if the affair should happen to be known, considerate people might be rather inclined to excuse an old woman, who would kindly take care of a young man, form his manners by her good counsels, and prevent his ruining his health and fortune among mercenary prostitutes.

5. Because in every animal that walks upright the deficiency of the fluids that fill the muscles appears first in the highest part. The face first grows lank and wrinkled; then the neck; then the breast and arms; the lower parts continuing to the last as plump as ever: so that covering all above with a basket, and regarding only what is below the girdle, it is impossible of two women to tell an old one from a young one. And as in the dark all cats are gray, the pleasure of corporal enjoyment with an old woman is at least equal, and frequently superior; every knack being, by practice, capable of improvement.

6. Because the sin is less. The debauching a virgin may be her ruin, and make her for life unhappy.

7. Because the compunction is less. The having mad a young girl miserable may give you frequent bitter reflection; none of which an attend the making an old woman happy.

8th and lastly. they are so grateful!!

Thus much for my paradox. But still I advise you to marry directly; being sincerely

Your affectionate friend,
B. Franklin

Apology for Printers

Ben Franklin was an early champion of freedom of the press. His focus on exposing multiple sides to issues and different points of view became the foundation for modern American journalism. He believed that the truth, even if unpopular, should be printed. On May 27, 1731, after being criticized for printing something contrary to the prevailing point of view, he responded by publishing the following "Apology" in *The Pennsylvania Gazette.*

Apology for Printers

Being frequently censur'd and condemn'd by different Persons for printing Things which they say ought not to be printed, I have sometimes thought it might be necessary to make a standing Apology for my self, and publish it once a Year, to be read upon all Occasions of that Nature. Much Business has hitherto hindered the execution of this Design; but having very lately given extraordinary Offence by printing an Advertisement with a certain "N.B." at the End of it, I find an Apology more particularly requisite at this Juncture, tho' it happens when I have not yet Leisure to write such a thing in the proper Form, and can only in a loose manner throw those Considerations together which should have been the Substance of it.

I request all who are angry with me on the Account of printing things they don't like, calmly to consider these following Particulars

1.   That the Opinions of Men are almost as various as their Faces; an Observation general enough to become a common Proverb, "So many Men so many Minds."

2.   That the Business of Printing has chiefly to do with Mens Opinions; most things that are printed tending to promote some, or oppose others.

3.   That hence arises the peculiar Unhappiness of that Business, which other Callings are no way liable to; they who follow Printing being scarce able to do any thing in their way of getting a Living, which shall not probably give Offence to some, and perhaps to many; whereas the Smith, the Shoemaker, the Carpenter, or the Man of any other Trade, may work indifferently for People of all Persuasions, without offending any of them: and the Merchant may buy and sell with Jews, Turks, Hereticks, and Infidels of all sorts, and get Money by every one of them, without giving Offence to the most orthodox, of any sort; or suffering the least Censure or Ill-will on the Account from any Man whatever.

4.   That it is as unreasonable in any one Man or Set of Men to expect to be pleas'd with every thing that is printed, as to think that nobody ought to be pleas'd but themselves.

5.   Printers are educated in the Belief, that when Men differ in Opinion, both Sides ought equally to have the Advantage of being heard by the Publick; and that when Truth and Error have fair Play, the former is always an overmatch for the latter: Hence they chearfully serve all contending Writers that pay them well, without regarding on which side they are of the Question in Dispute.

6. Being thus continually employ'd in serving all Parties, Printers naturally acquire a vast Unconcernedness as to the right or wrong Opinions contain'd in what they print; regarding it only as the Matter of their daily labour: They print things full of Spleen and Animosity, with the utmost Calmness and Indifference, and without the least Ill-will to the Persons reflected on; who nevertheless unjustly think the Printer as much their Enemy as the Author, and join both together in their Resentment.

7. That it is unreasonable to imagine Printers approve of every thing they print, and to censure them on any particular thing accordingly; since in the way of their Business they print such great variety of things opposite and contradictory. It is likewise as unreasonable what some assert, "That Printers ought not to print any Thing but what they approve;" since if all of that Business should make such a Resolution, and abide by it, an End would thereby be put to Free Writing, and the World would afterwards have nothing to read but what happen'd to be the Opinions of Printers.

8. That if all Printers were determin'd not to print any thing till they were sure it would offend no body, there would be very little printed.

9. That if they sometimes print vicious or silly things not worth reading, it may not be because they approve such things themselves, but because the People are so viciously and corruptly educated that good things are not encouraged. I have known a very numerous Impression of "Robin Hood's Songs" go off in this Province at 2"s". per Book, in less than a Twelvemonth; when a small Quantity of "David's Psalms" (an excellent Version) have lain upon my Hands above twice the Time.

10. That notwithstanding what might be urg'd in behalf of a Man's being allow'd to do in the Way of his Business whatever he is paid for, yet Printers do continually discourage the Printing of great Numbers of bad things, and stifle them in the Birth. I my self have constantly refused to print any thing that might countenance Vice, or promote Immorality; tho' by complying in such Cases with the corrupt Taste of the Majority, I might have got much Money. I have also always refus'd to print such things as might do real Injury to any Person, how much soever I have been solicited, and tempted with Offers of great Pay; and how much soever I have by refusing got the Ill-will of those who would have employ'd me. I have heretofore fallen under the Resentment of large Bodies of Men, for refusing absolutely to print any of their Party or Personal Reflections. In this Manner I have made my self many Enemies, and the constant Fatigue of denying is almost insupportable. But the Publick being unacquainted with all this, whenever the poor Printer happens either through Ignorance or much Persuasion, to do any thing that is generally thought worthy of Blame, he meets with no more Friendship or Favour on the above Account, than if there were no Merit in't at all. Thus, as "Waller" says,

"Poets loose half the Praise they would have got Were it but known what they discreetly blot;"

Yet are censur'd for every bad Line found in their Works with the utmost Severity.

I come now to the particular Case of the "N.B." above-mention'd, about which there has been more Clamour against me, than ever before on any other Account. -- In the Hurry of other Business an Advertisement was brought to me to be printed; it signified that such a Ship lying at such a Wharff, would sail for "Barbadoes" in such a Time, and that Freighters and Passengers might agree with the Captain at such a Place; so far is what's common: But at the Bottom this odd Thing was added, N.B. "No Sea Hens nor Black Gowns will be admitted on any Terms." I printed it, and receiv'd my Money; and the Advertisement was stuck up round the Town as usual. I had not so much Curiosity at that time as to enquire the Meaning of it, nor did I in the least imagine it would give so much Offence. Several good Men are very angry with me on this Occasion; they are pleas'd to say I have too much Sense to do such things ignorantly; that if they were Printers they would not have done such a thing on any Consideration; that it could proceed from nothing but my abundant Malice against Religion and the Clergy: They therefore declare they will not take any more of my Papers, nor have any farther Dealings with me; but will hinder me of all the Custom they can. All this is very hard!

I believe it had been better if I had refused to print the said Advertisement. However, 'tis done and cannot be revok'd. I have only the following few Particulars to offer, some of them in my Behalf, by way of Mitigation, and some not much to the Purpose; but I desire none of them may be read when the Reader is not in a very good Humour.

1.   That I really did it without the least Malice, and imagin'd the "N.B." was plac'd there only to make the Advertisement star'd at, and more generally read.

2.   That I never saw the Word "Sea-Hens" before in my Life; nor have I yet ask'd the meaning of it; and tho' I had certainly known that "Black Gowns" in that Place signified the Clergy of the Church of "England", yet I have that confidence in the

generous good Temper of such of them as I know, as to be well satisfied such a trifling mention of their Habit gives them no Disturbance.

3.   That most of the Clergy in this and the neighbouring Provinces, are my Customers, and some of them my very good Friends; and I must be very malicious indeed, or very stupid, to print this thing for a small Profit, if I had thought it would have given them just Cause of Offence.

4.   That if I have much Malice against the Clergy, and withal much Sense; 'tis strange I never write or talk against the Clergy my self. Some have observed that 'tis a fruitful Topic, and the easiest to be witty upon of all others. I can print any thing I write at less Charge than others; yet I appeal to the Publick that I am never guilty this way, and to all my Acquaintance as to my Conversation.

5.   That if a Man of Sense had Malice enough to desire to injure the Clergy, this is the foolishest Thing he could possibly contrive for that Purpose.

6.   That I got Five Shillings by it.

7.   That none who are angry with me would have given me so much to let it alone.

8.   That if all the People of different Opinions in this Province would engage to give me as much for not printing things they don't like, as I can get by printing them, I should probably live a very easy Life; and if all Printers were every where so dealt by, there would be very little printed.

9. That I am oblig'd to all who take my Paper, and am willing to think they do it out of meer Friendship. I only desire they would think the same when I deal with them. I thank those who leave off, that they have taken it so long. But I beg they would not endeavour to dissuade others, for that will look like Malice.

10. That 'tis impossible any Man should know what he would do if he was a Printer.

11. That notwithstanding the Rashness and Inexperience of Youth, which is most likely to be prevail'd with to do things that ought not to be done; yet I have avoided printing such Things as usually give Offence either to Church or State, more than any Printer that has followed the Business in this Province before.

12. And lastly, That I have printed above a Thousand Advertisements which made not the least mention of "Sea-Hens" or "Black Gowns"; and this being the first Offence, I have the more Reason to expect Forgiveness.

I take leave to conclude with an old Fable, which some of my Readers have heard before, and some have not.

"A certain well-meaning Man and his Son, were travelling towards a Market Town, with an Ass which they had to sell. The Road was bad; and the old Man therefore rid, but the Son went a-foot. The first Passenger they met, asked the Father if he was not ashamed to ride by himself, and suffer the poor Lad to wade along thro' the Mire; this induced him to take up his Son behind him: He had not travelled far, when he met others, who said, they were two unmerciful Lubbers to get both on the of that poor Ass, in such a deep Road. Upon this the old Man gets off, and let his Son ride alone. The next they met called the Lad a graceless, rascally young Jackanapes, to ride in that Manner thro' the Dirt, while his aged Father trudged along on Foot; and they said the old Man was a Fool, for suffering it. He then bid his Son come down, and walk with him, and they travell'd on leading the Ass by the Halter; 'till they met another Company, who called them a Couple of sensless Blockheads, for going both on Foot in such a dirty Way, when they had an empty Ass with them, which they might ride upon. The old Man could bear no longer; My Son, said he, it grieves me much that we cannot please all these People; Let us throw the Ass over the next Bridge, and be no farther troubled with him."

Had the old Man been seen acting this last Resolution, he would probably have been call'd a Fool for troubling himself about the different Opinions of all that were pleas'd to find Fault with him: Therefore, tho' I have a Temper almost as complying as his, I intend not to imitate him in this last Particular. I consider the Variety of Humours among Men, and despair of pleasing every Body; yet I shall not therefore leave off Printing. I shall continue my Business. I shall not burn my Press and melt my Letters.

An Address to the Public

In Franklin's later years, he wrote several essays on the importance of the abolition of slavery and the integration of blacks into American society, including this one from 1789:

An Address to the Public from the Pennsylvania Society for Promoting the Abolition of Slavery, and the Relief of Free Negroes Unlawfully Held in Bondage.

by Benjamin Franklin

It is with peculiar satisfaction we assure the friends of humanity, that, in prosecuting the design of our association, our endeavours have proved successful, far beyond our most sanguine expectations.

Encouraged by this success, and by the daily progress of that luminous and benign spirit of liberty, which is diffusing itself throughout the world, and humbly hoping for the continuance of the divine blessing on our labours, we have ventured to make an important addition to our original plan, and do therefore earnestly solicit the support and assistance of all who can feel the tender emotions of sympathy and compassion, or relish the exalted pleasure of beneficence.

Slavery is such an atrocious debasement of human nature, that its very extirpation, if not performed with solicitous care, may sometimes open a source of serious evils.

The unhappy man, who has long been treated as a brute animal, too frequently sinks beneath the common standard of the human species. The galling chains, that bind his body, do also fetter his intellectual faculties, and impair the social affections of his heart. Accustomed to move like a mere machine, by the will of a master, reflection is suspended; he has not the power of choice; and reason and conscience have but little influence over his conduct, because he is chiefly governed by the passion of fear. He is poor and friendless; perhaps worn out by extreme labour, age, and disease.

Under such circumstances, freedom may often prove a misfortune to himself, and prejudicial to society.

Attention to emancipated black people, it is therefore to be hoped, will become a branch of our national policy; but, as far as we contribute to promote this emancipation, so far that attention is evidently a serious duty incumbent on us, and which we mean to discharge to the best of our judgment and abilities.

To instruct, to advise, to qualify those, who have been restored to freedom, for the exercise and enjoyment of civil liberty, to promote in them habits of industry, to furnish them with employments suited to their age, sex, talents, and other circumstances, and to procure their children an education calculated for their future situation in life; these are the great outlines of the annexed plan, which we have adopted, and which we conceive will essentially promote the public good, and the happiness of these our hitherto too much neglected fellow-creatures.

A plan so extensive cannot be carried into execution without considerable pecuniary resources, beyond the present ordinary funds of the Society. We hope much from the generosity of enlightened and benevolent freemen, and will gratefully receive any donations or subscriptions for this purpose, which may be made to our treasurer, James Starr, or to James Pemberton, chairman of our committee of correspondence.

Signed, by order of the Society,

B. FRANKLIN, President.

Philadelphia, 9th of November, 1789

Epitaph

Franklin was buried beside his wife Deborah, who had died 25 years earlier. His son Francis Folger, who had died at age 4 from smallpox, was also in the family plot.

Although as a young man in 1728, Franklin had composed his own mock epitaph

The Body of
B. Franklin
Printer;
Like the Cover of an old Book,
Its Contents torn out,
And stript of its Lettering and Gilding,
Lies here, Food for Worms.
But the Work shall not be whlly lost:
For it will, as he believ'd, appear once more,
In a new & more perfect Edition,
Corrected and Amended
By the Author.
He was born on January 6, 1706.
Died 17

his gravestone simply reads:

BENJAMIN
And
DEBORAH FRANKLIN
1790

Turkey vs. Eagle

Although it has been often repeated, the story that Ben Franklin wanted the Turkey to be the national bird of the United States is not 100% true. Yes, once in writing he compared the two birds as symbols, but he never publically championed the Turkey as the symbol of America.

The story stems from a letter he wrote to his daughter Sarah Bache on January 26, 1784 (the Great Seal with the bald eagle as its centerpiece was adopted by Congress on June 20, 1782). In the letter he is criticizing the Society of the Cincinnati and in one section, he comments on the appearance of the Bald Eagle on their crest:

> *Others object to the Bald Eagle, as looking too much like a Dindon, or Turkey. For my own part I wish the Bald Eagle had not been chosen the Representative of our Country. He is a Bird of bad moral Character. He does not get his Living honestly. You may have seen him perched on some dead Tree near the River, where, too lazy to fish for himself, he watches the Labour of the Fishing Hawk; and when that diligent Bird has at length taken a Fish, and is bearing it to his Nest for the Support of his Mate and young Ones, the Bald Eagle pursues him and takes it from him.*

> *With all this Injustice, he is never in good Case but like those among Men who live by Sharping & Robbing he is generally poor and often very lousy. Besides he is a*

rank Coward: The little King Bird not bigger than a Sparrow attacks him boldly and drives him out of the District. He is therefore by no means a proper Emblem for the brave and honest Cincinnati of America who have driven all the King birds from our Country...

I am on this account not displeased that the Figure is not known as a Bald Eagle, but looks more like a Turkey. For in Truth the Turkey is in Comparison a much more respectable Bird, and withal a true original Native of America... He is besides, though a little vain & silly, a Bird of Courage, and would not hesitate to attack a Grenadier of the British Guards who should presume to invade his Farm Yard with a red Coat on.

THE "WORDS & WISDOM" SERIES

Available from Amazon.com and other retailers

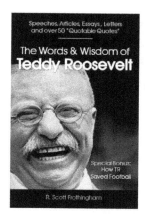
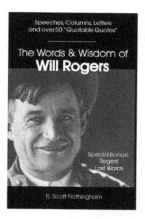

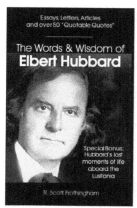

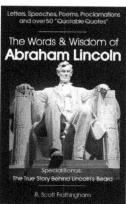

Selections of the actual words of historical figures
that will give you a better understanding of
the people behind the beloved icons and notable events.

ABOUT THE AUTHOR

Scott Frothingham is an entrepreneur, consultant, speaker, business coach and author best known for his FastForward Income™ products including *The 15-minute Sales Workout*™. He helps entrepreneurs, managers and sales/marketing executives position themselves for success through skills training and personal development -- along with providing tools for effectively and efficiently training and motivating their teams.

R. Scott Frothingham

www.ScottFrothingham.com

Facebook: **www.Facebook.com/FastForwardIncome**

Twitter: **@ScottFroth**

www.FastForwardPublishing.com

Edward S. Ellis is best known for his youth-targeted fictional works in the American dime, pulp, and series novel genre like *Seth Jones* or *The Captives of the Frontier* (described as the "perfect dime novel" of thrilling frontier adventure -- estimated 60,000 copies in its first week and 450,000 copies in its first six months), *The Huge Hunter* or *The Steam Man of the Prairies* (first U.S. science fiction dime novel) and the series featuring Native American: Deerfoot. Later in life he turned to more serious work, writing accounts of historical events and biographies, mostly for adults.

For more details on the life, career and books of Edward S. Ellis, visit **www.EdwardSEllis.com**.

www.FastForwardPublishing.com

CPSIA information can be obtained
at www.ICGtesting.com
Printed in the USA
BVHW041301020719
552491BV00016B/178/P